A Taste of

Marijuana

Summer Fun

Cookbook

By Gracie and Sam

Copyright

We dedicate this book in loving
memory of Tom, and of Wayne.
We miss you both.

Disclaimer

Any decision to add medical marijuana to your
food is strictly your own.

We do not suggest anyone engage in any activity
that might violate the laws of the state or
country in which he or she lives.

Current news reports say the use of illegal
marijuana is contributing to increased violence
in North America.

We must work together with our elected officials
to come up with a solution.

Marijuana use may impair your co-ordination,
and thus is not advised for driving or
operating heavy machinery.

The amount the body can tolerate varies with
each individual.

Acknowledgements

We'd like to thank our friends and family for their input, patience, love and support. Special thanks to BMW, Bronco, Fenrin, Junior, Pat-I and White Oak.

ALSO BY GRACIE AND SAM

A TASTE OF MARIJUANA:

WINTER HOLIDAY COOKBOOK

A Taste of Marijuana: Summer Fun

Table of Contents

Introduction

These recipes were created for the fun and enjoyment of preparing and consuming medicinal marijuana.

We have a little bit of something for everyone. There are recipes for the non-vegetarian, vegetarian and vegans alike.

Feel free to use your own favorite recipes and substitute infused ingredients.

The recipes will stand on their own if you choose to make them without infused ingredients for your herb free guests.

For those who are not familiar with natural foods, you may use your own ingredients.

We find that food is much more flavorful and satisfying when whole grain and organic ingredients are used.

Marijuana can be used in any of your favorite recipes by adding infused ingredients and/or the powdered herb (flowering bud).

Fats or alcohol must be used to extract the medicinal and psychoactive properties.

We accomplish this by infusing the herb into alcohol, oils, butter and other dairy products.

Use the infusions in baked goods, sauces, gravies and casseroles, or any of your favorite recipes.

Making infusions and always having them on hand makes it easy to create a recipe at any time.

These fabulous recipes are some of Gracie's favorites from her 34 years of vegetarian cooking.

Hemp or Marijuana:
It's all Cannabis

Cannabis and its uses have been around for
thousands of years.

It is grown for two different purposes, industrial
hemp and medical marijuana.

Hemp is grown for the fiber, which is woven into
cloth for clothing and canvas. Hemp fiber was
routinely used in the paper making industry.
The seeds are used for their oil content and as a
high protein, high fiber source of food.

Marijuana is grown for its medicinal and
psychoactive properties.

The medical use of cannabis is mentioned in most
ancient and medieval medicinal texts.

(3000 B.C.) China grew and harvested
the cannabis plant "ta ma".
The seed was used for oil and food.
The fiber was used for clothing, sails and nets,
way back then.

The ancient manuscript "Pen Ts' ao" and the
sixteenth century manuscript "Pen Ts'ao Kang
Mu" discussed the many uses of hemp.

Ancient Chinese physician "Hoa-Gho" mixed the
resin with wine to use as an anesthetic in surgery.

Portuguese physician "Garcia da Orta" (1502-1568) bred several strains of resinous cannabis and wrote a scientific treatise on its therapeutic uses.

"The Complete Herbal", published in 1645, summarized the medicinal uses of cannabis.

The 1794, Edinburgh New Dispensatory, notes treatments using hempseed oil in milk.

Louis Aubert-Roche wrote a book in 1840 on his investigations into cannabis.

In 1842, surgeon William B. O'Shaughnessy brought the telegraph to India and cannabis to Britain.

Moslem sailors routinely used cannabis for seasickness.

Infused Butter

There are three methods of preparing infused butter.

Strained Butter: Has a mild nutty marijuana flavor. This is the least potent of the three methods of infusing and has a light green color.

Partially Strained Butter: Has a stronger flavor and potency. The added herb makes for a darker green color and more texture.

Water method: Makes an even stronger potency, but no buttery flavor.

Strained Butter
2 sticks organic butter*
6 Tbl finely powdered herb

Simmer on very low in a heavy, covered pot for 30-60 minutes.
For stronger potency, cook an additional 30-60 minutes.
Stir occasionally to prevent butter from burning.
Let cool.
Stir cooked butter, and strain through a fine sieve into a storage container.
Use a rubber spatula to press out all the butter to get every last drop.
Butter is ready to use right away.
Cover and refrigerate for future use.
You may also save the strained herb.

Don't wash your utensils just yet.
Use the leftover infused remnants of butter that are on the strainer and in the pot for marijuana gravy (see sam's marijuana gravy pg 49).

Partially Strained Butter
Follow the directions for strained butter.
Add 1 to 2 Tbl strained infused herb back to the
butter for more potency, color, texture and flavor.
Or you may leave unstrained and use as is.

Water method
2 sticks organic butter*
3 qts of pure water
6 Tbl finely powdered herb

3 Tbl = 1/8 oz. = 3 1/2 gm.
In a large pot, melt butter and stir in herb.
Add water and mix well, bring to a boil.
Reduce heat to a low boil and cover.
Cook for 6 hours.
Check hourly and add water as needed.
Partially cool and refrigerate overnight.
The butter will float to the top and become solid.
Remove butter to a clean container.
Discard water and solids.

*Vegans may substitute 16 Tbl of coconut oil for
the two sticks of butter.

Use strained or partially strained butter on:
Breads, dinner rolls, and garlic bread.
Baked or mashed potatoes.
Over steamed vegetables or popcorn.
Breakfast toast, pancakes, toaster waffles and
french toast.

Use in cooking:
Eggs, omelets, sautéed vegetables, stir-fry's,
sauces, gravies, soups, stews, and in baking.

Infused Oils

Flax, Hemp or Olive

Pour 1 cup of your choice of oil into a clean glass
bottle.
Add 4 tsp finely ground herb.
Shake three times daily for 3-5 days, keep
refrigerated.
For a stronger infusion wait 7-9 days.
Strain through a fine sieve and return oil to a
clean bottle. Keep refrigerated.

Flax and hemp seed oils are a source of omega 3-
6-9s, protein, soluble and insoluble fiber.
Olive oil is a beneficial mono-saturated fat.

Stir 1 Tbl infused flax or hemp oil into:
1 cup (8 oz.) of salsa, guacamole, salad dressing,
yoghurt, cottage cheese, sour cream, cream cheese
or mayonnaise.
Nut butters, bean dip, hummus, sauces and
gravies.
Easily added to shakes and smoothies.

Use infused olive oil:
Drizzle on garlic bread.
Add to pasta sauce, salad dressings and vegetable
side dishes.

Variation:
You may add 2 Tbl of finely ground herb to your
favorite bottle of organic salad dressing.
Shake three times daily for 3-5 days.
Keep refrigerated.

APPETIZERS

Centennial Celery Sticks

1 half bunch organic celery
8 oz. organic cream cheese*
4 tsp infused flax or hemp oil (see infused oils pg 7)
1/2 tsp sea salt
1/2 tsp garlic powder
1/2 tsp onion powder
Scant pinch of cayenne pepper
Natural blue food coloring**
Natural red food coloring**

Soften cream cheese. Place cream cheese, oil and spices in a bowl, mix well.
Chill for 1 hour to infuse flavors.

For red, white and blue:
Separate the mixture into three separate bowls.
Add blue food coloring to one, red food coloring to another, and leave the third plain white.
Stir each well.

Wash and slice celery into 3 inch pieces on the diagonal.
Spread alternating colors on the diagonal, 1 inch red, 1 inch white, and then 1 inch blue.
Repeat for each piece.

*Vegans may substitute non-dairy cream cheese.

** We enjoy using natural food colorings, but with white foods like cream cheese and sour cream, the red and blue turns out pink and lavender. For true red and blue, you may want to use artificial food coloring.

Patriotic Onion Dip

Yield: 2 cups

2 cups sour cream
2 Tbl infused oil (see infused oils pg 7)
3 Tbl dried onion flakes
2 tsp tamari
1 tsp garlic powder
1 tsp dill
1/2 tsp onion powder
1/2 tsp sea salt
Dash cayenne
Natural red food coloring*
Natural blue food coloring*

In a mixing bowl add oil to sour cream, stir.
Add remaining ingredients, except the red and
blue food coloring, stir.
Chill for 1 hour to infuse flavors.

For red, white and blue dip:
Separate the mixture into three separate bowls.
Add red food coloring to one, blue food coloring
to another, and leave the third plain white.
Mix each well, dollop all 3 into one serving bowl.
Serve with organic potato chips.

Summer time saver:
Stir 2 Tbl infused oil (see infused oils pg 7) into
16 oz. sour cream, and add one package onion
soup mix.

* We enjoy using natural food colorings, but with
white foods like cream cheese and sour cream, the
red and blue turns out pink and lavender. For true
red and blue, you may want to use artificial food
coloring.

Yankee Doodle Bean Dip

Serves 6-8

1 (16 oz.) can organic refried beans
2 Tbl infused butter (see infused butter pg 5)
1 1/2 cup organic cheddar cheese, grated
1 cup infused salsa (see fiesta salsa pg 14)
1 cup organic sour cream
1 cup infused guacamole (see guacamole pg 13)
2 cups shredded lettuce
3/4 cup chopped green onions

In a separate bowl, mash infused butter into the
beans and mix well.
Spread a layer of beans in the bottom of an 8 x 8
inch square baking dish.
Sprinkle grated cheese on top.
Pour salsa over cheese, evenly.
Spoon sour cream on top of salsa.
Top with guacamole.
Add shredded lettuce and chopped onions.

Serve with red, white and blue corn chips,
available at your favorite health food store.

Summer time saver:
Purchase organic salsa and add 1 Tbl infused oil
per 8 oz. (see infused oils pg 7).

Purchase organic guacamole and add 1 Tbl
infused oil per 8 oz. (see infused oils pg 7).

Hum Us a Tune
(Hummus Dip)

Yield: 2 cups

1 (15 oz.) can garbanzo beans
1 Tbl infused butter (see infused butter pg 5)
2 Tbl infused oil (see infused oils pg 7)
1 lg clove organic garlic
2 Tbl fresh organic lemon juice
2 Tbl tahini
1 Tbl tamari
1/4 tsp sea salt
2 Tbl fresh parsley or 1 Tbl dried parsley
1/2 tsp cumin

Put garlic in food processor and chop.
Add the rest of the ingredients and blend together.
Scrape down with rubber spatula and blend again.

Serving suggestion:
Can be used in sandwich wraps (see sandwich wraps pg 73), and as a party dip served with red, white and blue corn chips.

Summer time saver:
Purchase organic hummus and add 1 Tbl infused oil per 8 oz. (see infused oils pg 7).

Guacamole

Yield: 2 cups

2 lg ripe avocadoes
4 tsp infused flax or hemp oil (see infused oils pg 7)
2 tsp fresh lemon or lime juice
1/4 tsp sea salt
1/4 tsp garlic powder
1/8 tsp coriander
1/8 tsp cumin
Small pinch cayenne powder

Cut avocado in half.
Remove pit with a spoon.
Scoop out into a bowl.
Mash thoroughly with a fork until creamy.
Add oil, lemon juice, salt, garlic powder,
coriander, cumin, and cayenne powder.
Stir with a spoon and serve.

Serve with red, white and blue corn chips
available at your favorite health food store.

Summer time saver:
Purchase organic guacamole and add 1 Tbl
infused oil per 8 oz. (see infused oils pg 7).

Fiesta Salsa

Yield: 4 cups

1 (28 oz.) can organic diced tomatoes, with juice
4 med cloves organic garlic
1/4 cup fresh cilantro
1/4 cup chopped onion
1/4 cup chopped green pepper
1 tsp infused olive oil (see infused oils pg 7)
1 tsp infused flax or hemp oil (see infused oils pg 7)
1 tsp sea salt
Pinch cayenne
Juice of 1 lime

Chop garlic and cilantro in a food processor.
Scrape down with a rubber spatula.
Add the rest of the ingredients and pulse several times.

Serve with red, white and blue corn chips available at your favorite health food store.

Summer time saver:
Purchase organic salsa and add 2 Tbl infused oil per 16 oz. (see infused oils pg 7).

Party Pesto

Yield: 1 cup

4 cups organic fresh spinach
2 cups of fresh basil
Juice of 1/2 organic lemon
3 cloves of garlic
1/2 cup pine nuts
1/2 cup pecans
1/2 cup infused olive oil (see infused oils pg 7)
1/2 tsp sea salt

Put garlic in food processor and chop.
Add the rest of the ingredients and blend together.
Scrape sides down with rubber spatula and blend
again.

As an appetizer:
Serve with raw veggie rounds, celery sticks or
baby carrots.
Also goes well with whole grain or gluten free
crackers and chips.

As an entrée:
Serve over whole grain, gluten-free or raw
vegetable pasta (see raw vegetable pasta pg 75).

Serving suggestion:
Can be used in sandwich wraps (see sandwich
wraps pg 73) and raw wraps (see raw lettuce
wraps pg 74).

Patio Pate

1 Tbl miso
1 rounded Tbl raw almond butter
1 Tbl raw sesame tahini
1 tsp infused organic flax or hemp oil
(see infused oils pg 7)
1/2 inch piece of peeled fresh ginger, minced
2 cloves garlic, minced

In a small bowl, stir the miso, almond butter,
tahini and oil together.
Add ginger and garlic, blend well.

Spread on raw veggie rounds, celery sticks or
baby carrots.
Goes well with whole grain or gluten-free
crackers, or chips.

*You may use dark or light miso.

Absolutely Artichokes

Serves 6

6 fresh organic artichokes
1 stick (1/2 cup) of infused organic butter (see
infused butter pg 5)
1 tsp garlic powder
Dash of sea salt

With a scissor, cut off the sharp tip of each leaf
all the way around the artichoke.
Cut off the bottom stem.
Steam artichokes in a large covered pot for 30-40
minutes, until leaves pull off easily.
Melt butter.
Add garlic powder and salt.
Stir well.
Pour the butter mixture into 6 small bowls.
Place each butter bowl on a plate with 1 artichoke,
for each guest.
Dip each leaf individually in butter.
Pull leaf through your teeth to separate the pulp
and butter from the skin.
Repeat and enjoy.

SUMMER SALADS

Presidential Potato Salad

Serves 4

4 cups cooked organic potatoes, cut into
1 inch pieces
1/2 cup organic onion, chopped small
1/4 cup organic celery, chopped small
1/4 cup organic green pepper, chopped small
1 1/2 cup natural mayonnaise
2 Tbl infused oil (see infused oils pg 7)
1 Tbl organic mustard
3/4 tsp sea salt
1/2 tsp pepper
1/4 tsp garlic powder

Boil potatoes until cooked, but not too soft.
(approx. 20-25 minutes).
Drain water and let cool.
In a medium mixing bowl, stir together the
mayonnaise, oil, mustard and spices.
Add onion, celery and green pepper.
Mix well.
Add potatoes and stir gently to mix evenly.
Cover and refrigerate at least 1/2 hour to blend
flavors.

Garnish with a parsley sprig and cherry tomato.

You may double or triple the recipe for large
parties.

Picnic Pasta Salad

1 (8 oz.) box whole grain or gluten-free elbow
pasta
1 Tbl infused butter (see infused butter pg 5)*

Boil water for pasta.
Add infused butter.
Cook according to directions.
Drain pasta and set aside to cool.

1 3/4 cup natural mayonnaise
2 Tbl infused oil (see infused oils pg 7)
1 tsp sea salt
1/2 tsp pepper
1 tsp garlic powder
3/4 cup black olives, halved
1/3 cup onion, chopped small
1/3 cup green pepper, chopped small
1/2 cup celery, chopped small

In a large mixing bowl, add oil to mayonnaise and
stir.
Add spices and vegetables, stir again.
Gently fold in pasta and mix well.
Refrigerate at least 1 hour to infuse flavors.

* Vegans may substitute infused oils (see infused
oils pg 7).

Union Tuna Salad

Serves 6

1 (12 oz.) can wild caught, dolphin safe tuna
1 cup natural mayonnaise
1 Tbl infused oil (see infused oils pg 7)
1/3 cup celery, chopped small
3/4 tsp sea salt
1/2 tsp garlic powder
1/4 tsp pepper
Small pinch of cayenne

Drain tuna and place in a medium mixing bowl.
Flake with a fork to separate.
Stir in mayo, oil, celery and spices.
Mix well.

Serve on whole grain or gluten-free crackers, or as
a sandwich with whole grain or gluten-free bread.

Confederate Cole Slaw

Serves 4

2 cups organic cabbage, shredded
1/4 cup onion, grated
1 small carrot, grated
3/4 cup natural mayonnaise
2 Tbl infused flax oil (see infused oils pg 7)
1/4 cup currants
1/8 tsp sea salt
1/8 tsp pepper

Cut cabbage head into quarters and core.
Slice each quarter thinly to shred.
Cut onion into quarters.
Hold one quarter firmly, and grate using a cheese grater.
Grate the carrot.
Put vegetables in a medium mixing bowl.
Add remaining ingredients.
Stir to mix well.
Cover and refrigerate 1 hour to infuse flavors.

Easy Egg Salad

4 organic free-range eggs
1/3 cup natural mayonnaise
1 Tbl infused oil (see infused oils pg 7)
1 tsp mustard
1/2 tsp sea salt
1/4 tsp pepper
1/4 tsp garlic powder
Small pinch cayenne

Hard boil eggs for 7 minutes.
Soak in cold water 2-3 minutes, and drain.
Peel, rinse and shake dry.
Place in a mixing bowl.
Chop with a fork and a knife into small chunks.
Add mayonnaise, oil, mustard, salt, pepper, garlic
powder and cayenne.
Mix well.

Serve on your favorite whole grain or gluten-free
bread.

For garnish:
Nestle radish or tomato wedges in a sprig of
parsley.

Cucumbers and Sour Cream

1 lg cucumber
16 oz. organic sour cream
4 tsp infused oil (see infused oils pg 7)
1 tsp tamari
1 tsp garlic powder
1 tsp dill
¼ tsp sea salt
¼ tsp pepper

Slice peeled organic cucumber into a dish or
container.
Add oil, tamari, and spices to sour cream.
Mix well.
Pour over cucumbers and toss lightly.
Chill before serving.

Rabbit Munchies
(A.K.A. Tossed Salad)

1 head romaine or leaf lettuce
1 vine ripe organic tomato
1 lg carrot
1/2 red bell pepper
1/2 orange bell pepper
3/4 cup purple cabbage
1/2 medium cucumber
1 stalk celery
2 Tbl salad sprinkles (see salad sprinkles pg 27)
1 cup salad dressing
1 Tbl infused oil (see infused oils pg 7)

Pour oil into salad dressing, shake well.
Gently tear lettuce leaves into a large salad bowl.
Slice carrots into match stick size pieces.
Cut bell peppers into match stick size pieces.
Chop cabbage into thin slices.
Score cucumber with a fork.
Slice and chop into bite size pieces.
Thinly slice celery on the diagonal.
Chop tomato into bite size pieces.

Add vegetables to lettuce and gently toss.

Top with salad sprinkles and salad dressing.

Cool as a Cucumber Salad

Serves 6

2 med organic tomatoes
1 lg cucumber
1 cup chopped fresh basil, chopped
1/4 cup infused oil (see infused oils pg 7)
1 tsp tamari
1/2 tsp sea salt
1/4 tsp pepper
1 Tbl salad sprinkles (see salad sprinkles pg 27)

Use chilled tomatoes and cucumber.
Slice tomatoes.
Score the cucumber with a fork.
Slice cucumber.
Alternate slices of tomato and cucumber on
individual salad plates.
Top with chopped basil.
Combine oil, tamari and spices.
Mix well.
Drizzle oil over all.

Top with salad sprinkles to serve.

Salad Sprinkles

2 Tbl sesame seeds
2 Tbl sunflower seeds
3 Tbl sliced or slivered almonds
1 Tbl hemp seeds

Pre-heat skillet to medium-hot.
Add sesame seeds.
Shake pan and stir occasionally to toast evenly.
Seeds will begin to pop when done (approx. 3-5 min).
Empty into a bowl.
Add sunflower seeds and toast until very light brown (approx. 2 min).
Empty into same bowl.
Add almonds and toast carefully until light brown (approx. 1 min).
Empty into same bowl.
Add untoasted hemp seeds.
Stir.

Note:
Hemp seeds are small, flat white seeds. These are the seeds that are used in food preparation.

Valley Forge
Vinaigrette Dressing

Yield: 1 cup

1/2 cup infused extra virgin olive oil (see infused
oils pg 7)
1/4 cup fresh organic lemon juice
1 Tbl fresh organic lime juice
1/4 tsp dry mustard
1 Tbl fresh parsley, finely chopped
or 1 tsp dried parsley
Dash garlic powder
Dash sea salt
Small pinch cayenne

Whisk, shake or blend to mix.
Chill 1 hour to infuse flavors.
Shake and serve.

Mid-Summer
Miso Dressing

Yield: 1 1/4 cups

1 cup infused organic vegetable oil (see infused
oils pg 7)
2 Tbl fresh organic lemon juice
2 Tbl tamari
2 Tbl minced onion
1 Tbl honey
1/4 cup white or golden miso*
Dash cayenne

Combine all ingredients in a blender and blend on
high speed for 1 minute.
Scrape down sides and blend for another minute.
Thin with water if necessary.

*Miso is a naturally salty soybean paste with
alkalizing mineral salts (see natural ingredients).

Colorado Mayo

1/3 cup natural mayonnaise
1/2 tsp infused oil (see infused oils pg 7)
1/2 tsp tamari
1/2 tsp nutritional yeast

Mix all ingredients together in a small bowl.

Use as a quick sauce, dip, or sandwich spread.

Serving suggestion:
Excellent as a sauce mixed with chopped raw
vegetables and served in pita bread.

Note:
The unique flavor combination in this recipe is far
superior using natural mayonnaise.

When Gracie and Sam lived in Colorado, this was
one of their first flavor combinations that showed
them how good and flavorful natural foods can be.

Breads And Desserts

13 Colonies Corn Bread

Serves 4 to 6

1 cup cornmeal
1 cup organic whole grain or gluten-free flour
5 tsp baking powder
3/4 tsp sea salt
1 cup organic or non-dairy milk
1 lg organic free-range egg, beaten
2 Tbl infused butter, melted (see infused
butter pg 5)
2 Tbl honey

Preheat oven to 375°F.
In a mixing bowl combine cornmeal, flour, baking
powder, and salt.
In a separate bowl, whisk together milk, egg,
butter and honey.
Pour wet ingredients into the dry ingredients and
beat 50 strokes with a wooden spoon.
Pour into an oiled 9 x 9 inch pan, bake 30
minutes.
Check with a toothpick.
Edges should be slightly brown.
Serve warm with butter and honey.
Goes great with Habanero Chili (see habanero
chili pg 55).

Options:
Add 1/4 cup chopped green chilies
or 1/4 cup chopped green pepper.

For orange cornbread, add 2 tsp grated orange
peel.

Summer time saver: Buy natural cornbread mix,
and follow directions using infused ingredients.

Gracie's Garlic Bread

Whole grain or gluten-free bread
3 Tbl infused butter (see infused butter pg 5)*
3 Tbl non-infused butter
3-4 cloves garlic, minced
Pinch of sea salt

Melt butter.
Mince garlic, you may use a garlic press.
Add garlic to butter and cook on low for 5
minutes, stirring occasionally.
Add sea salt and stir.
Use a spoon to drizzle butter on toasted bread.

*Vegans may substitute infused olive oil.

Banana Bread

1 1/4 cup organic whole grain flour
1 cup unbleached white or brown rice flour
3 1/2 tsp baking powder
3/4 tsp sea salt
1/3 cup infused butter, melted (see infused butter pg 5)
3/4 cup honey
2 organic free-range eggs
1 1/4 cups mashed ripe organic bananas
1 cup chopped walnuts

Preheat oven to 350°F.
In bowl combine flour, baking powder and salt.
Set aside.
In a large mixing bowl combine butter, honey and eggs.
Add flour mixture alternately with bananas, a small amount at a time.
Beat well after each addition.
Fold in nuts.
Turn into a well-oiled loaf pan and bake 1 hour and 10 minutes.
Cool slightly before removing from pan.

Frost with Freedom Frosting (see freedom frosting pg 41).

Summer time saver:
Buy whole grain natural banana bread mix and follow directions using infused ingredients.

Fab Fruit

4 organic pears
4 Tbl infused butter, melted (see infused
butter pg 5)
4 Tbl non-infused butter, melted
2 Tbl honey
1 Tbl maple syrup
2 tsp cinnamon

Wash, core and thinly slice pears.
Cut slices in half.
Place in a mixing bowl.
In a medium pan, melt butter.
Add honey, maple syrup, and cinnamon.
Stir to mix well.
Add sliced fruit.
Stir gently.
Simmer for 5 minutes.
Scoop into individual serving dishes.
Serve and enjoy.

Serve warm or room temperature.

You may substitute apples, peaches, apricots or
berries.

Beach Peach Cobbler

Serves 6-8

Fruit Filling
 6-8 ripe organic peaches, skinned
1/4 cup honey
2 tsp cinnamon

Wash and peel peaches.
Slice thinly into a well-oiled 9 x 13 inch baking dish.
Drizzle honey over peaches.
Sprinkle with cinnamon.
Toss gently to mix.

Topping
1 cup whole grain flour
1/2 cup unbleached white or brown rice flour
1cup organic rolled oats
1 cup organic brown sugar
1/2 tsp sea salt
1/2 tsp cinnamon
1/4 tsp allspice
1/4 tsp nutmeg
1/8 tsp cloves
1/2 tsp baking soda
4 Tbl infused butter, cold (see infused butter pg 5)
4 Tbl non-infused butter, cold

Cobbler instructions

Preheat oven to 350°F.
Combine flours, oats, brown sugar and spices in a separate mixing bowl.
Mix well.
Knead the butter into the flour mixture with your fingers to make small crumbles.
Top peaches evenly with crumble mixture.
Bake 45-55 minutes until crust is golden brown.
Let cool.
Serve warm or cold.
Top with organic whipped cream or natural ice cream.

Washington's Apple Crisp

You may substitute 6-8 organic apples.
Use same ingredients and directions as Beach Peach Cobbler.

Blitzen Brownies

2 cups organic brown sugar
3 organic free-range eggs
1 tsp vanilla
1/2 cup infused organic butter
(see infused butter pg 5)
1 cup whole grain or gluten-free flour
1/2 cup unbleached white or brown rice flour
3/4 cup cocoa powder
2 tsp baking powder
1/2 tsp sea salt
2 rounded Tbl finely powdered herb
3/4 cup organic pecans and/or walnuts, chopped
small
3/4 cup chocolate chips

Preheat oven to 350°F.
Cream the butter and brown sugar together.
Add vanilla and eggs.
Beat with an electric mixer until light.
Mix dry ingredients together in a separate bowl,
including the herb.
Add dry ingredients to butter mixture and blend
with mixer or stir 50 strokes with a wooden
spoon.
Add nuts and chocolate chips.
Stir with a heavy spoon.
Turn into a well-oiled, 9 x 13 baking pan.
Spread evenly.
Bake at 350°F for 25-30 minutes.
Cool before cutting into squares.

Frost with Freedom Frosting (see freedom
frosting pg 41) for a 4th of July flair.

For added texture and marijuana flavor, use partially strained butter (see infused butter pg 5).

Summer time saver:
Buy whole grain natural brownie mix and follow directions using infused ingredients.

Blitzen Brownies is borrowed from "A Taste of Marijuana: Winter Holiday Cookbook".

Freedom Frosting

Yield: 2 1/2 cups

16 oz. organic cream cheese
6 Tbl infused butter (see infused butter pg 5)
6 Tbl non-infused butter
2 tsp vanilla extract
8 Tbl maple syrup
Natural red food coloring*
Natural blue food coloring*

Soften cream cheese to room temperature.
Add butter and mash together.
Stir in vanilla and maple syrup, mix well.

Divide the mixture into three bowls.
1/3 cup frosting for blue.
1/2 cup each for red and white.
Add the blue food coloring to one, mix well.
Add the red food coloring to another, mix well.
Leave the 3rd bowl white.

To decorate a 9 x 13 cake like an American flag:
Spoon each color into separate plastic bags.
For blue, cut a small hole in one corner of the plastic bag.
Squeeze blue onto the top left corner of the cooled brownies or cake.
Spread with a knife to form a square.
Cut a very small hole in the corner of the white bag.
Squeeze small stars onto the blue square.

Cut a small hole in the corner of the red bag.
There are 7 short red and white stripes to the right
of the blue square. The remaining 6 long stripes
go all the way across.
Starting at the top, to the right of the blue square,
squeeze your first red stripe.
Alternate white and red for the first 7 short
stripes, ending with red.
For the last 6 long stripes start with white, then
red, alternating and ending in red.

* We enjoy using natural food colorings, but with
white foods like cream cheese and sour cream, the
red and blue turns out pink and lavender. For true
red and blue, you may want to use artificial food
coloring.

Chocolate Frosting

Yield: 1 1/3 cup

8 oz. organic cream cheese
3 Tbl infused butter (see infused butter pg 5)
3 Tbl non-infused butter
1/2 tsp vanilla extract
7 Tbl maple syrup
1/2 cup cocoa powder

Soften cream cheese and butter to room
temperature.
Place in a deep mixing bowl and beat with an
electric mixer.
Scrape down sides with a rubber spatula.
Add vanilla and maple syrup, beat again.
Sprinkle in cocoa powder, slowly.
Beat until creamy.
Scrape down sides and beat again.

You may double the recipe to cover a 9 x 13 inch
cake.

Chocolate Fudge

Yield: 16 small squares

1/3 cup infused organic butter (see infused butter pg 5)
1 cup chocolate chips
1/2 tsp vanilla
1 Tbl small bud crumbles
1 Tbl toasted sliced almonds

Melt butter on low in small sauce pan.
Add small bud crumbles, not finely powdered.
Simmer on low for 5 minutes, stirring occasionally.
Add chocolate chips and simmer to melt, stir frequently.
Add vanilla and sliced almonds.
Stir and let cool a few minutes.
Stir and pour into a small square dish.
Stir again and refrigerate.
After 5 minutes remove from refrigerator and stir well.
Return to refrigerator and let harden.
Cover to store.
Let soften and cut into squares.
A 5 x 5 inch dish makes 16 small squares.

You may double or triple the recipe and cut into larger pieces.

SIDE DISHES

Rosemary Bud Spuds

Serves 6

18 small organic red potatoes
1/3 cup infused olive oil (see infused oils pg 7)
6 cloves garlic, peeled and coarsely chopped
1 Tbl chopped fresh rosemary
1/2 tsp sea salt

Preheat the oven to 350 ° F.
Cut potatoes in half.
In a large bowl stir the rosemary, garlic and salt
into the oil.
Add potatoes and toss well to coat.

Place the potatoes in a shallow baking dish and
bake until tender.
Test with a fork.
Approximate cooking time 30-40 minutes.

Broccoli Baked Potatoes

Serves 4

4 lg organic baking potatoes
1/4 cup organic almond milk
2 cups broccoli florets, steamed
1 cup organic cheddar cheese, grated
Sea salt and freshly ground pepper to taste
4 Tbl infused butter (see infused butter pg 5)

Preheat oven to 400° F.
Bake potatoes for 1 hour or until done.
Let cool and cut each in half, length wise.
Scoop out the inside of each potato half with
a spoon, leaving a shell about 1/4 inch thick.
Put the shells aside.
Place the potato pulp into a mixing bowl.
Mash coarsely with a fork.
Add the milk, broccoli, cheese, butter, salt, and
pepper.
Mix well.
Spoon the mixture into the potato shells.
Place on a baking sheet.
Bake for 15 minutes until hot.
Salt and pepper to taste.

Sam's Marijuana Gravy

1 1/2 cups pure water
1/2 tsp sea salt
1/2 tsp garlic powder
1 Tbl plus 1 tsp arrowroot powder
1 Tbl tamari

Use the leftover infused remnants of butter that are on the strainer and in the pot from making infused butter (see infused butter pg 5).

Boil water.
Slowly pour the boiling water through strainer into the butter pot.
Stir and scrape pot with a rubber spatula to incorporate all the butter.
Add salt and garlic powder, stir.
Heat water on med-low heat, bring to a slow boil.
Put arrowroot powder into a coffee mug and add some of the heated water.
Stir to mix, and add back to the water in butter pot.
Stir almost continuously, and bring to a boil.
Cook for a few minutes as gravy thickens.
Add tamari, stir, and remove from heat.

You may use the butter water like any other water or stock to make soup, gravy, stew or to parboil veggies.

For turkey gravy, check out "A Taste of Marijuana: Winter Holiday Cookbook."
See Turkey Marijuana Gravy.

Rainbow Quinoa

Serves 4-6

1 cup quinoa
2 cups pure water
1/4 tsp sea salt
1/2 medium purple onion, finely chopped
1/4 cup finely chopped carrots
1/3 cup red bell pepper, seeded and finely chopped
1/3 cup green bell pepper, seeded and finely chopped
1 tsp olive oil
2 Tbl infused butter (see infused butter pg 5)
2 Tbl salad sprinkles (see salad sprinkles pg 27)
2 Tbl chopped fresh cilantro
2 tsp tamari

Rinse quinoa well.
Boil 2 cups of water in a medium pan.
Add quinoa and salt.
Bring to a boil again.
Reduce heat to low.
Cover and cook for 15 minutes.

Heat oil in a medium skillet.
Add butter to melt.
Sauté onion for 10 minutes.
Add carrots, cover and cook for 5 minutes.
Add peppers, stir, cover and cook for 5 minutes.
Add quinoa, salad sprinkles, cilantro and tamari.
Stir gently to mix well.

Vegetable Variety

Steamed carrots

Serves 4
4 medium carrots
2 Tbl infused butter (see infused butter pg 5)*

Wash carrots and slice on the diagonal.
Steam for 10 minutes, until tender.
Drain and return to pot.
Add butter, stir and serve.

Green Beans

Serves 4
3 cups fresh green beans
2 Tbl infused butter (see infused butter pg 5)*
2 tsp tamari

Wash and snip off ends.
Cut beans into thirds on the diagonal.
Steam 10-15 minutes till tender-crisp.
Drain and return to pot.
Add butter and tamari.
Stir and serve.

Summer time saver:
Use 1 (10 oz.) package frozen green beans. Cook
according to directions to make 3 cups cooked
green beans.

* Vegans may substitute infused oils (see infused
oils pg 7).

Broccoli and Cauliflower

Serves 4
3 cups organic broccoli, florets
3 cups organic cauliflower, florets
2 Tbl infused butter (see infused butter)*
1 Tbl tamari
1 Tbl nutritional yeast flakes

Wash cauliflower.
Cut into quarters.
Cut out the core.
Break into florets.
Place cauliflower in steamer and cover.
Steam for 5 minutes.
In the meantime, wash broccoli, cut off stem and break into florets.
Add broccoli to steamer.
Stir vegetables to mix.
Cover and steam 10-15 minutes until tender-crisp.
Test with a fork.
Drain and remove vegetables from pot.
Add butter to pot to melt.
Stir in tamari and nutritional yeast.
Mix well.
Add vegetables and stir to coat.

*Vegans may substitute infused oils (see infused oils).

Cheesy Zucchini and Tomatoes

Serves 4

1 med organic onion, sliced
2 small organic zucchini, sliced
2 med vine-ripe tomatoes, sliced
1/4 tsp sea salt
1/4 tsp basil
1 tsp garlic powder
1 cup whole grain or gluten-free croutons
1 cup organic cheese, shredded
3 Tbl infused butter (see infused butter pg 5)

Melt butter in a large skillet.
Add onions and cook covered for 5 minutes.
Add zucchini, stir, cover and cook 5 minutes.
Add tomatoes and seasonings, gently stir.
Cover and cook 4 minutes.
Remove from heat, and sprinkle croutons and
cheese over vegetables evenly.
Cover and let stand until cheese is melted.

MAIN DISHES

Habanero Chili

TVP*
1 cup TVP granules
Scant 1 cup water
3 Tbl organic vegetable oil
2 Tbl infused butter (see infused butter pg 5)
1 Tbl tamari

Boil water, turn off heat, and add tamari.
Place TVP in a mixing bowl, add water, and stir.
Let set for 15 minutes, stirring occasionally.
The TVP will absorb the water and fluff up.
In the meantime, heat medium skillet.
Add oil and butter to melt.
Add TVP and cook 10-15 minutes, stirring
occasionally, until browned.
Set aside and let cool.

*You may substitute 2 cups of cooked
free-range ground turkey.

Chili

3 Tbl infused organic butter (see infused
butter pg 5)
2 Tbl organic vegetable oil
1 large onion, cut in quarters, then thinly sliced
1 green pepper, diced
1 (4 oz.) can diced green chilies
3 cloves garlic, minced
1/4 cup chili powder
1/4 cup cumin
2 tsp sea salt
1 fresh habanero pepper, finely minced or 1/8 to
1/4 tsp cayenne powder. Use gloves.

1 (25 oz.) can organic kidney beans, un-drained
1 (28 oz.) can organic whole peeled tomatoes,
with juice
1 (28 oz.) can organic diced tomatoes, with juice
2 Tbl tamari

Chili Instructions

In a large pot, heat oil and butter to melt.
Sauté onions for 30 minutes covered, on low
until translucent, stirring occasionally.
Add green pepper, stir and cook covered for 10
minutes.
Add garlic and spices, cover and cook 5 minutes
more.
Add green chilies and tamari.
Stir, cover and cook 5 minutes.
Add the canned tomatoes and kidney beans.
Stir in TVP and simmer covered for 1/2 hour.

Top with local organic grated cheese and a dollop
of sour cream.

Serve with whole grain crackers topped with
infused butter (see infused butter pg 5).

For milder chili use 3/4 of a minced habanero or
1/8 tsp cayenne powder.

Note: TVP is textured vegetable protein made
from soy beans. It is sold in crumbles (like
ground beef) or in cubes. Buy the crumbles for
this recipe.

Summer time saver:
Purchase already prepared vegetarian crumbles.
You'll find them in the freezer section.

Sloppy Janes

Serves 4-6

TVP*
1 1/2 cups TVP
Scant 1 1/2 cup pure water
3 Tbl organic vegetable oil
2 Tbl infused butter (see infused butter pg 5)
1Tbl tamari

Boil water, turn off heat, and add tamari.
Place TVP in a mixing bowl, add water and stir.
Let set for 15 minutes, stirring occasionally.
The TVP will absorb the water and fluff up.
In the meantime, heat medium skillet.
Add oil and butter to melt, add TVP.
Cook 10-15 minutes, stirring occasionally until
browned. Set aside and let cool.

*You may substitute 2.5 cups of cooked
free-range ground turkey.

Sauce
1/2 med onion, diced
3/4 med green pepper, diced
1 Tbl vegetable oil
3 Tbl infused organic butter (see infused
butter pg 5)
2-3 garlic cloves, minced
1/3 cup ketchup
2 Tbl mustard
1/2 cup BBQ sauce
1 Tbl tamari
1/2 cup water
1 tsp sea salt
1/2 tsp pepper

Sloppy Jane Instructions

Heat oil and butter to melt.
Add onion and sauté for 10 minutes, covered.
Add green pepper and cook 5 minutes, covered.
Add garlic and cook 3 minutes, covered.
Add ketchup, mustard, BBQ sauce, tamari, water,
salt and pepper.
Mix well.
Add TVP and stir.
Simmer for 5 minutes, covered.

To serve:
Top whole grain or gluten free bread, or buns,
with the hot sloppy jane mix.
Sprinkle organic grated cheese on top if desired.

Note:
TVP is textured vegetable protein made from soy
beans. It is sold in crumbles (like ground beef) or
in cubes. Buy the crumbles for this recipe.

Summer time saver:
Purchase already prepared vegetarian crumbles.
You'll find them in the freezer section.

Turkey Tetrazzini

Serves 4

2 cups cooked turkey, cut into 1-2 inch chunks
3/4 cup onion, chopped
1 lg clove garlic, minced
1 Tbl parsley
1 Tbl strained herb (see infused butter pg 5)
1/2 tsp sea salt
1/4 tsp pepper
1 Tbl organic vegetable oil
2 Tbl infused butter (see infused butter pg 5)
2 rounded Tbl whole grain flour*
1 Tbl nutritional yeast
1 cup non-dairy milk
1 cup frozen peas, thawed
1 Tbl tamari
1 cup organic cheddar cheese, grated

Heat oil in a large sauce pan and add butter to melt.
Add onion, cover and sauté 10 minutes on low heat until onions are soft.
Add garlic, parsley, strained herb, salt and pepper.
Stir, cover and cook another 5 minutes.
Sprinkle in flour, stir continuously for 2 minutes.
Add nutritional yeast and stir.
Add tamari to milk and slowly pour into pan.
Stir continuously to prevent lumps.
Add peas and turkey, and cook another 10 minutes on low, stirring occasionally.
Stir in grated cheese and cook another 2 minutes to melt the cheese.

Turkey Tetrazzini - continued

* You may substitute millet, flax seed or chia seed flour. Millet flour is Gracie's favorite high protein, gluten-free alternative to wheat flour. Flax and chia seed flour are great thickeners too. See Natural Ingredients pages (pg 87-90) for more information.

Tempeh Teriyaki

1 (8 oz.) pkg tempeh, cut into ¼ inch strips
1 Tbl organic vegetable oil
2 Tbl infused butter (see infused butter pg 5)
1 Tbl tamari

Heat oil in a large skillet, and add butter to melt.
Fry tempeh 4-5 minutes on each side, until crisp.
Remove tempeh from skillet and drain on paper
towels.
Drain excess oil from skillet and return to heat.
Add tempeh back to skillet.
Sprinkle with tamari.
Cook 1 minute on each side to sear.
Remove tempeh and set aside.

1 med onion, thinly sliced
1 lg green pepper, cut in thin strips
1 pint mushrooms, sliced
1 Tbl organic vegetable oil
2 Tbl infused butter (see infused butter pg 5)
1 Tbl tamari
1/2 of a 10 oz. bottle natural teriyaki sauce

Heat oil in a large skillet and add butter to melt.
Sauté onions 10 minutes, covered.
Add green pepper and mushrooms, cook 10
minutes, covered.
Remove vegetables from skillet and drain on
paper towels.
Drain excess oil.
Put vegetables in a small mixing bowl.
Add tamari and teriyaki sauce.
Stir to mix well.

Tempeh Teriyaki - continued

Serve over brown rice, (see stir fry vegetables over rice pg 67) or serve over whole grain or gluten-free ribbon noodles, or egg noodles.

To assemble:
Place rice or pasta on dinner plates.
Top with vegetables and then tempeh strips.
Drizzle extra teriyaki sauce over each plate.

Tofu Parmesan

Serves 4

Pasta
1 (8 oz.) box whole grain or gluten-free elbow pasta
1 Tbl infused butter (see infused butter pg 5)
Boil water for pasta.
Add infused butter.
Cook according to directions.
Drain pasta and set aside to cool.

Breaded Tofu
1 lb firm tofu, drained on paper towels
1 cup organic corn meal
2 Tbl grated parmesan cheese
1 Tbl garlic powder
1 Tbl onion powder
1/2 tsp sea salt
1/2 cup organic vegetable oil
2 Tbl infused butter (see infused butter pg 5)
8 oz. organic mozzarella cheese, grated

Combine corn meal, spices, and parmesan cheese in a shallow bowl or plate.
Cut Tofu into 1/4 inch slices.
Coat tofu slices, one at a time with corn meal mixture on both sides.
Heat oil in a large skillet, and add butter to melt.
Fry in hot oil until brown on both sides.
Lay on paper towels to dry.

Sauce

1 jar organic pasta sauce
1/4 onion, chopped small
3 cloves garlic, minced
1 Tbl parsley
1 Tbl finely powdered herb
2 tsp oregano
1 Tbl infused butter (see infused butter pg 5)
1 Tbl infused olive oil (see infused oils pg 7)

Sauté onion in oil and butter for 10 minutes.
Add garlic and herbs.
Cook 5 more minutes, stirring occasionally.
Add sauce, stir, and simmer for 15 minutes on low.

Option: Use 2 Tbl finely powdered herb for higher potency.

Pre-heat oven to 350° F.
Oil a 9 x 13 inch baking dish.
Spoon 3/4 cup pasta sauce into the bottom of baking dish.
Arrange tofu in pan, and add 1 cup more sauce.
Top with grated cheese.
Bake at 350° until hot and cheese is melted, about 20 minutes.

Serve on a plate over pasta, and shake some parmesan on top of all.

Serve with garlic bread (see gracie's garlic bread pg 34) and salad (see rabbit munchies pg 25).

Tofu Stew

Serves 4-6

1 (14 oz.) container firm tofu
6 small organic red potatoes, quartered
1 lg onion, cut in 1 inch chunks
2 lg carrots, cut in half lengthwise and cut
into 1/2 inch pieces
2 stalks celery, sliced diagonally into 1/2 inch
pieces
4 garlic cloves, minced
2 Tbl organic vegetable oil
3 Tbl infused butter (see infused butter pg 5)
3 Tbl tamari
2 tsp sea salt
1 Tbl parsley
1 tsp marjoram
2 vegetable bouillon cubes
1/4 cup whole grain flour*
4 cups pure water
2 Tbl strained herb (see infused butter pg 7)

Cut tofu into 1 inch cubes.
Steam for 15 minutes (otherwise the tofu will
crumble).
Drain.
Place into a medium bowl.
Add 2 Tbl tamari and stir gently with a spoon to
coat all pieces.
Set aside.

Stew Instructions

Boil potatoes in a pot of water until just soft.
Drain and set aside to cool.
In a large pot, heat oil and butter.
Add onions, stir, cover, and cook on medium low
for 10 minutes.
Add carrots, stir, cover, and cook 5 minutes,
stirring occasionally.
Add celery, stir, cover, and cook 10 minutes.
Add garlic, parsley, marjoram, strained herb, salt
and bouillon cubes.
Stir, cover, and cook for 5 minutes more.
Sprinkle in flour, stirring constantly to make a
roux.
Stir continuously for 2 minutes.
Add water slowly, stirring continuously to avoid
lumps.
Turn up heat.
Bring to a quick boil while stirring occasionally.
Reduce heat to low.
Add potatoes, tofu, and remaining 1 Tbl tamari.
Stir gently.
Simmer uncovered for 15 minutes, stirring
occasionally.

* You may use millet, flax seed or chia seed flour.
Millet flour is Gracie's favorite high protein,
gluten-free alternative to wheat flour. Flax and
Chia seed flour are great thickeners. See Natural
Ingredients pages (pg 87-90) for more
information.

Stir-fried Vegetables over Rice

2 lg organic carrots
1 large broccoli stalk
1/2 head of cauliflower
1 green pepper
2 stalks celery
1 medium organic onion
1 large yellow squash or zucchini
1/2 small head red cabbage
2 Tbl safflower or peanut oil
2 Tbl infused butter (see infused butter pg 5)
2 Tbl tamari
1 tsp powdered ginger
1/2 tsp garlic powder

Cut carrots on the diagonal into 1/2 inch pieces.
Remove broccoli stem and cut top into bite-size florets.
Cut the 1/2 head of cauliflower in half, remove core.
Break into bite-sized florets.
Core green pepper and cut into 1 inch pieces.
Cut celery stalks on the diagonal into 1/2 inch slices.
Cut onion into 1 inch pieces.
Remove ends of squash or zucchini, slice in half length-wise.
Lay on flat side, and slice into 1/2 inch half-moon pieces.
Cut the 1/2 head of cabbage in half, remove core.
Chop into 1 inch pieces.
Heat oil in a large skillet or wok, over medium heat. Add butter.

Add carrots, broccoli, and cauliflower, stir.
Cover and cook for 7 minutes, stirring frequently.
Add green pepper, celery, onion, zucchini and
cabbage, stir.
Cover and cook an additional 8-10 minutes.
Turn heat up, and add tamari, ginger and garlic
powder.
Stir, tossing vegetables to coat.
Cook 1 minute.

Rice
1 cup organic brown rice
2 cups plus 1 Tbl water
1 vegetable bouillon cube
1 Tbl infused butter (see infused butter pg 5)

Rinse rice in strainer.
Combine rice, water, butter and bouillon in pot
with lid.
Bring to a boil, stir once, cover.
Turn heat down to low and cook 50 minutes.
Remove from heat, let stand 10 minutes.

To serve:
Place warm, cooked brown rice on a dinner plate.
Top with a good serving of stir-fried vegetables.
Drizzle a little tamari over each plate.

Excellent Enchiladas

Serves 4

8 organic corn tortillas
1 (16 oz.) can organic refried beans
3 Tbl infused butter, softened (see infused butter pg 5)
1 (15 oz.) can green chile enchilada sauce
1/2 cup organic black olives, chopped
8 oz. organic grated jack and/or cheddar cheese, grated*
4 oz. organic cream cheese, softened*
1/2 cup organic onions, minced
Shredded organic lettuce
1 med organic vine ripe tomato, chopped small
8 oz. organic sour cream
1 Tbl infused oil (see infused oils pg 7)*
Infused salsa (see fiesta salsa pg 14)
Infused guacamole (see guacamole pg 13)

Preheat oven to 375°F.
Oil a 9 x 13 inch glass baking dish.
Place beans and butter in a food processor, blend.
Scrape sides down with rubber spatula, and blend again.
Stir oil into sour cream.
Refrigerate until ready to use.
Lay out 8 tortilla shells.
Spoon some beans along the middle of each shell.
Spread a line of cream cheese alongside the beans.
Sprinkle each with some of the grated cheese and onions.

Spoon 1 Tbl enchilada sauce over each tortilla shell.

Pour 1 cup of enchilada sauce into the bottom of an oiled baking dish.

Roll each enchilada, and place in a row in baking dish on top of sauce.

Pour rest of the enchilada sauce over all, covering evenly.

Top with remaining grated cheese.

Sprinkle remaining onions evenly over cheese.

Sprinkle olives over all.

Cover with foil.

Bake for 25 minutes.

Remove foil.

Return to oven and bake an additional 10 minutes.

*Vegans may substitute non-dairy grated cheese, cream cheese and sour cream.

Serving suggestion:

Place 2 enchiladas on an individual dinner plate.

Top with lettuce and tomatoes.

Top with a dollop each of sour cream, guacamole and salsa.

Summer time saver:

Purchase organic salsa and add 1 Tbl infused oil per 8 oz. (see infused oils).

Purchase organic guacamole and add 1 Tbl infused oil per 8 oz. (see infused oils).

Tasty Tacos

Buffet style

12 organic Non-GMO taco shells or flat tostada
shells
1 (16 oz.) can organic refried beans
16 oz. organic sour cream
2 cups infused guacamole (see guacamole pg 13)
8 oz. organic jack and/or cheddar cheese, grated
Shredded lettuce and/or green cabbage
3/4 cup chopped onion and/or green onion
1 1/2 cups chopped tomato
4 Tbl infused flax or hemp oil (see infused
oils pg 7)
Natural red food coloring*
Natural blue food coloring*
Infused salsa (see fiesta salsa pg 14)

Place beans into a bowl. Stir in 2 Tbl oil and mix
well.
In separate bowl, stir 2 Tbl oil into sour cream.

Divide sour cream into three equal parts and place
in separate bowls.
Stir red food coloring into one bowl, mix well.
Stir blue food coloring into another bowl, mix
well.
Leave the 3rd bowl white.

Toast shells in oven on high, or below the broiler,
for 2-3 minutes until lightly golden.
Place on a serving plate.

Put beans, salsa, guacamole and grated cheese in their own individual bowls, with serving utensils. Arrange lettuce, onion and tomatoes on a plate.

Assemble your tacos and top with a small dollop each of red, white and blue sour cream.

* We enjoy using natural food colorings, but with white foods like cream cheese and sour cream, the red and blue turns out pink and lavender. For true red and blue, you may want to use artificial food coloring.

Sandwich Wraps

6 whole grain burrito shells
1 1/2 cup infused hummus dip (see hum us a tune
pg 12)
1 1/2 cup organic jack or cheddar cheese, grated*
2 cups lettuce, thinly chopped
3/4 cup green onions, chopped
1 lg vine ripe tomato, chopped
3/4 cup green pepper, chopped

Lay out burrito shells.
Spread 3 rounded Tbl of hummus along the
middle of each shell.
Top with lettuce.
Sprinkle 1/4 cup cheese.
Top with onions, tomato and green pepper.
Roll, slice in half on the diagonal and serve.

As an appetizer: Roll wraps and cut into 1 inch
pieces and serve on a party platter. Garnish platter
with colorful veggies like cherry tomatoes,
radishes or baby carrots. Nestle in parsley sprigs
or green-leafy lettuce leaves.

Serving option: Wrap your favorite fillings in
lettuce or cabbage leaves (see raw lettuce wraps
pg 74).

*Vegans may substitute non-dairy cheese.

Summer time saver:
Purchase organic hummus and add 1 Tbl infused
oil per 8 oz. (see infused oils pg 7).

Raw Lettuce Wraps

Serves 4

8 lg leaves organic romaine lettuce or cabbage
Infused pesto (see party pesto pg 15)
3/4 cup green onion, chopped
3/4 cup vine ripe tomato, chopped
3/4 cup organic cucumber, chopped

Rinse lettuce leaves.
Lay out lettuce leaves.
Spoon 1-2 Tbl pesto lengthwise along the center
of each leaf.
Sprinkle onion, tomato and cucumber over all.
Roll up lengthwise, and secure with toothpicks.
Slice in half on the diagonal.
Serve 2 wraps per person.

Garnish platter with colorful veggies like cherry
tomatoes, radishes, carrot and cucumber sticks.
Nestle in parsley sprigs.

For variety:
Substitute hummus dip (see hum us a tune pg 12)
for the pesto. Hummus is made with cooked
garbanzo beans, so the dish will no longer be
completely raw.

Raw Vegetable Pasta

Serves 4-6

1 lg carrot
1 lg zucchini
1 lg yellow summer squash
1 med green pepper
1 med red pepper
1 cup infused pesto (see party pesto pg 15)

Peel off the outer layer of the carrot with a potato peeler, and compost or discard.
Using the potato peeler, peel the entire carrot and save into a medium mixing bowl.
Cut off tips of the zucchini.
Using the potato peeler, peel the zucchini down to the seeds and save into the same mixing bowl.
Cut off the tips of the squash.
Using the potato peeler, peel the squash down to the seeds and save into the same mixing bowl.
Slice peppers in half and discard core and seeds.
Julienne (slice thinly) peppers, and save into the same mixing bowl.
Gently toss to mix well.
Divide onto 4-6 dinner plates.
Top each with a large dollop of pesto.

This recipe should be served immediately after cutting the vegetables.

Option:
Use a raw food spiral slicer to make angel hair pasta with the carrots, zucchini and yellow squash.

Outdoor Grilling Fun

Summer isn't complete without
cooking and eating outdoors.

Top your favorite organic meats or vegetarian
burgers and hot dogs with infused condiments.

Set out separate dishes of mayo, ketchup, and
mustard.

Add 1 Tbl of infused oil (see infused oils pg 7) for
every cup of condiment.

Use infused ingredients in your favorite marinade.

Serve with Presidential Potato Salad (pg 19), or
any of the many summer salads in this cookbook.

Add infused ingredients to a whole grain or
gluten-free cake mix and top with chocolate
frosting (see chocolate frosting pg 43).

Or design a flag with Freedom Frosting (see
freedom frosting pg 41) for your
4th of July spread.

See Campfire Food (pg 78) for additional ideas to
preparing foods in foil on the grill.

Campfire Food

Food cooked around the campfire is the best.

There are many camping foods that you can either put in the campfire coals or cook on the grill.

The following are just a few ideas of the many you can do to infuse some fun into your outdoor cooking.

Camping Breakfast Potatoes (pg 79)

Roasted Onions and Garlic (pg 80)

Roasted Vegetables (pg 81)

Fireside Fish (pg 82)

Baked Potatoes (pg 83)

Roasted Garlic (pg 84)

Marinated Tofu Shish-Kabob (pg 85)

Camping Breakfast Potatoes

Bake the potatoes in the campfire the night before.
(see campfire food-baked potatoes pg 83)

4 med-lg pre-baked potatoes
3-4 Tbl organic vegetable oil
3 Tbl infused butter (see infused butter pg 5)
1/2 med onion
1/2 lg green pepper
6 lg mushroom buttons, chopped
2 tsp sea salt
1 tsp pepper
1 cup organic jack or cheddar cheese, grated*
Organic ketchup
Natural steak sauce

Dice potatoes 1/4 inch thick.
Dice onion and green pepper.
Heat oil in a large skillet, on medium heat.
Add butter to melt.
Add potatoes, cook 5 minutes.
Add onions and green peppers, cook 8 minutes.
Add mushrooms and cook another 2-3 minutes
until potatoes are nicely browned.
Top with salt, pepper and grated cheese.
Remove from heat, and cover to melt cheese.

To serve:
Sprinkle ketchup and steak sauce over each
potato.

*Vegans may substitute non-dairy cheese.

These are great served at home at the breakfast
table.

Roasted Onions and Garlic

1 lg onion, sliced thin
4 cloves garlic, chopped coarsely
3 Tbl infused butter (see infused butter pg 5)
1 Tbl Tamari

Place vegetables in foil.
Add butter and seal.
Wrap in 2nd layer of foil.
Seal securely.
Bake in the coals around the perimeter
of the campfire.
Turn often to bake evenly and prevent
burning.
Cook 15-20 minutes.
Open foil carefully to avoid steam.
Check with a fork.
Add tamari.
Serve.

Roasted Vegetables

4 cups of chopped vegetables
3 pats of infused butter (see infused butter pg 5)
1 Tbl tamari

Place chopped vegetables in foil.
Add butter and seal.
Wrap in a 2nd layer of foil.
Seal securely.
Bake in the coals around the perimeter
of the campfire.
Turn often to bake evenly and prevent burning.
Cook 15-20 minutes.
Open foil carefully to avoid steam.
Check with a fork.
Add tamari.
Serve.

Fireside Fish

4 fresh med fish fillets
8 pats of infused butter (see infused butter pg 5)
1 Tbl parsley
1 tsp garlic powder
1 tsp sea salt
½ tsp pepper
Vegetable oil

Combine parsley, garlic powder, sea salt and
pepper in a bowl.
Coat the inside of 4 pieces of foil with oil.
Place each fillet on the foil.
Sprinkle with spices.
Place 2 pats of butter on each fillet.
Wrap the fillets in a second piece of foil.
Seal securely.
Bake in the coals around the perimeter
of the campfire.
Turn often to bake evenly and prevent burning.
Cook approximately 10-15 minutes.
Be careful not to overcook.
Open foil carefully to avoid steam
and check for doneness.

Top with onions and garlic (see campfire food-
roasted onions and garlic pg 80).

Serve with potatoes (see campfire food-baked
potatoes pg 83) and vegetables (see campfire
food-roasted vegetables pg 81).

Baked Potatoes

Baking potatoes
1 1/2 Tbl of infused butter (see infused
butter pg 5) per potato

Place potato in foil.
Add butter and seal.
Wrap in 2nd layer of foil.
Seal securely.
Bake in the coals around the perimeter of the
campfire.
Turn occasionally to bake evenly and prevent
burning.
Cook approximately 1 hour.
Check after 45 minutes.
Cooking time varies.
Bake until cooked but not overdone.

Top with infused butter, sea salt and pepper.

Top with infused sour cream. Stir 1 Tbl infused
oil (see infused oils pg 7) into 8 oz. sour cream.

Summer time saver:
Cut and prepare your vegetables at home.
Wash, prepare and wrap your potatoes in foil, at
home.

Roasted Garlic

6 whole organic garlic bulbs
1/4 cup infused olive oil (see infused oil pg 7)
Pinch of sea salt

Brush bulbs with oil.
Wrap each bulb in a double layer of foil, and seal
securely.
Bake in the coals around the perimeter
of the campfire.
Turn often to bake evenly.
Cook 15-20 minutes.
Open foil carefully to avoid steam.
Squeeze bulb to check.
It is done when soft.
Let cool slightly.
Squeeze garlic out onto whole grain or gluten-free
crackers.
Top with sea salt.

Marinated Tofu Shish-Kabob

1 (14 oz.) container, firm to extra firm tofu, marinated*
1 can organic pineapple chunks
1 lg organic onion
1 lg organic zucchini
1 pint organic cherry tomatoes
2 lg organic carrots
2 lg organic green peppers
Infused olive oil (see infused oils pg 7)
Sea salt and pepper

*Marinade-prepare the night before.
4 cups pure water
1/4 cup tamari
2 tsp garlic powder
2 tsp ginger powder

In a medium bowl, combine water and tamari.
Add garlic powder and ginger, stir.
Cut tofu into 1 inch squares.
Add tofu and turn gently with a spoon to coat.
Cover and refrigerate overnight.

When ready to prepare meal, drain tofu and steam for 10 minutes.
Steaming will firm tofu to keep from crumbling.

After steaming tofu, drain and set aside.
Cut off ends of carrots.
Slice into 1 inch pieces, on the diagonal.
Steam 5 minutes, to partially cook.

Cut onion into 2 inch chunks.
Cut green peppers into 2 inch pieces.
Cut off ends of zucchini.
Cut into 2 inch chunks.
Use metal or wooden skewers.

To assemble:
Start with a piece of carrot.
Then skewer a piece of tofu, green pepper,
pineapple, onion, zucchini and tomato.
Repeat ending with a cherry tomato and add a
carrot.
Starting and finishing with a hard vegetable, like a
carrot, will help hold it together.

Brush with olive oil to coat.
Sprinkle on salt and pepper to taste.
Place on grill, cover, and cook.
Turn every few minutes.
Done when vegetables are soft.

Natural Ingredients

For our friends who aren't as familiar with the natural terms and ingredients used in this cookbook.

Almond flour: High in vitamin E, folic acid and minerals. A grain-free choice.

Almond milk: Non-dairy milk made from almonds. Thicker than rice milk, and a delicious alternative to soy milk.

Amaranth: Is a tiny seed, smaller than quinoa. It is a complete protein grain.

Arrowroot powder: An easily digested, low carb, starch thickener. Great for sauces, soups, gravies and fruit fillings. Also used as an egg replacement.

Brown rice: The whole grain, still containing the fiber and nutrients that are removed in the refining process. High in fiber, B vitamins and minerals.

Chia seeds: When ground into flour it is an excellent thickener for soups, stews, sauces, gravies and desserts. Chia is a rich source of omega 3's and dietary fiber. Also contains more anti-oxidants that blueberries and six times more calcium than milk.

Flax seed: Abundant in omega 3 fatty acids, lignans and dietary fiber. Provides all ten essential amino acids (complete protein).
Great source of trace vitamins and minerals.

Flax flour: A high protein, high fiber flour. Great for thickening soups, sauces and gravies.

Flax oil: A source of omega 3-6-9s, protein, soluble and insoluble fiber.

Free-Range Poultry: Allowed to roam outdoors and are fed natural feed.

Gluten-Free: Contains no gluten. Gluten is a protein found in wheat, barley and rye. It can be highly allergenic.

Grass-fed: Cattle are allowed to roam free and eat the natural grasses according to nature's laws.

Hemp: Complete protein. High in soluble and insoluble fiber, balanced source of omega 3-6-9 fatty acids.

Hemp flour: Protein rich, gluten-free, whole grain flour that has a nutty flavor. It is a bit grainy, so use only a small portion in your recipe.

Hemp oil: A source of omega 3-6-9s, protein, soluble and insoluble fiber.

Millet: A small round yellow grain with a distinct sweet flavor. A good source of protein, essential amino acids and fiber. It is gluten-free and easily digested.

Miso: A thick, naturally fermented paste made from soybeans, rice and/or barley. It is high in protein and rich in vitamins and minerals. Makes a wonderful stock for soups and gravies, and can be used to make spreads and pate`s.

Naturally refined cooking oils: Are processed without the use of any harsh chemicals or contaminants and can be used for cooking at higher temperatures.

Non-Dairy Milk: Can be made from almonds, hemp seeds, rice, table nuts and soy.

Non-GMO (genetically modified organisms): Not modified on a genetic level, deviating from nature.

Nutritional yeast flakes (not powder): Has a nutty roasted flavor. The yeast provides complete protein, lots of B vitamins and minerals. This is not a baking yeast.

Olive oil (Extra virgin): High in important monosaturated fats. Has a mild olive flavor.

Organic Produce: Grown according to nature in high nutrient soil without the use of herbicides, pesticides and fungicides.

Organic Butter: Butter made from the milk of free range grass-fed cows.

Organic Dairy: Products made from free-range grass-fed cows.

Peanut oil: This oil has a high smoke point, making it ideal for stir-fry's, sauté's and other high heat recipes.

Quinoa: A tiny grain, light tan in color, the same size as millet. It is a complete protein grain that supplies all of the essential amino acids. A very good source of magnesium, and is gluten-free.

Quinoa flour: Has a stronger, more robust grain flavor.

Safflower oil: This oil has a high smoke point making it ideal for stir-fry's, sauté's and other high heat recipes. Has a neutral flavor.

Sea Salt: Natural sea salt has 92 essential minerals. Refined salt is a by-product of the chemical industry which contains only 2 elements, sodium and chlorine. Salt, in its natural state, is essential to basic cellular health.

Tahini (Sesame Butter): Made from ground sesame seeds. An excellent source of calcium, iron and B vitamins.

Tamari: A naturally brewed soy sauce that provides much less sodium than table salt.

Tempeh: A fermented soybean cake often used as a vegetarian meat substitute. High in protein, low in sodium, and a good source of calcium and iron.

TVP (Textured vegetable protein): A granulated soy product used as a vegetarian meat substitute.

Unbleached White Flour: Is partially refined whole wheat, and still has some fiber and nutrients in it. Also, it is not bleached like white flour is.

Unrefined oil: The nutrients and unique flavors are not lost in processing. An example would be extra virgin olive oil.

Vine Ripe Tomato: Allowed to ripen on the vine, thus developing full nutrient content and flavor.

Whole grain: Contains vitamins, minerals, trace minerals and fiber. Refining removes most of these nutrients. Some examples are amaranth, brown rice, chia, millet, quinoa and wheat.

Whole grain flour: There is a variety of whole grain flours, now available, to choose from. They include brown rice, chia, flax, hemp, millet, quinoa and whole wheat.

Whole wheat: High in fiber, B vitamins and minerals. High in gluten, an allergen for many people. Great for thickening soups, sauces and gravies.

Wild caught / Dolphin Safe Tuna: Caught in the open ocean in its natural habitat, using dolphin safe fishing methods.

Closing Comments

Using organic and naturally processed ingredients makes a big difference in our personal health and the health of our planet.

Natural, plant based cleaning supplies are another way to reduce our carbon footprint.

We purchase our dairy products, eggs and poultry from local farmers who use natural feed and free-range practices.

Shopping at locally-owned markets and frequenting restaurants that support local vendors and farmers is another way to keep our money in our own community.

We support globally responsible companies.

How our dollars are spent speaks volumes by showing support for the company or industries whose products we purchase.

If we don't like certain practices, we don't purchase their products.

We hope you enjoy preparing and consuming these Summer Fun creations.

Have a Happy, Healthy,
Herb Holiday

From Gracie and Sam